TOSEL®

READING SERIES

HIGH JUNIOR

READING

3

KB158117

ITC International TOSEL Committee

CONTENTS

About TOSEL®

TOSEL (Test of Skills in the English Language) was developed to meet the demand for a more effective assessment of English as a foreign language for learners from specific cultural settings.

TOSEL evaluates and certifies the proficiency levels of English learners, from the age of 4 through adulthood, along with academic and job performance results.

Background

- Other English tests are ineffective in accurately measuring individual abilities
- Overuse of US-dominated testing systems in diverse cultural and educational contexts in the global English language learning market

Functions & Usage

- Assessment is categorized into 7 levels
- Used as a qualification for academic excellence for school admissions
- Used as a test to assess the English proficiency in the corporate and public sectors

Goals

- Create an effective tool for assessing and evaluating the English skills of English language learners
- Implement efficient and accessible testing systems and methods
- Provide constructive and developmental English education guidance

TOSEL® Strength

LEVELED ASSESSMENTS

An established English test system fit for seven different levels according to learners' cognitive development

ACCURATE DIAGNOSIS

A systematic and scientific diagnosis of learners' English proficiency

EXTENSIVE MATERIALS

Supplementary materials to help learners in an EFL environment to prepare for TOSEL and improve their proficiency

SUFFICIENT DATA

Content for each level developed by using data accumulated from more than 2,000,000 TOSEL test takers delegated at 15,000 schools and academies

CLASSIFIED AREAS OF INTELLIGENCE

Content designed to foster and expand the strengths of each student, categorized by the eight areas of intelligence

CONTINUITY

A complete course of English education ranging from kindergarten, elementary school, middle school, high schoool, and up to adults.

HIGH RELIABILITY

A high reliability level (Cronbach's alpha: .904 for elementary school students / .864 for university students) proven by several studies (Oxford University / Modern Language Journal)

SYSTEMATIC & EFFECTIVE ENGLISH EDUCATION

Accurate diagnosis and extensive materials which provide a step-by-step development in English learning, according to the quality of each learner's ability

TOSEL® Level Chart

Seven Separate Assessments

TOSEL divides the test into seven stages, by considering the test takers' cognitive levels, according to different ages. Unlike other assessments based on only one level, TOSEL includes separate assessments for preschool, elementary school, middle school, high school students, and for adults, which also includes both professionals and college students.

TOSEL's reporting system highlights the strengths and weaknesses of each test taker and suggests areas for further development.

COCOON

Suitable for children aged 4-6 (pre-schoolers)

The first step in the TOSEL system, the test is composed of colorful designs and interesting questions to interest young learners and to put them at ease.

Pre-STARTER

Suitable for children aged 7-8 (1st-2nd grades of elementary school)

Evaluates the ability to comprehend simple vocabulary, conversations, and sentences.

STARTER

Suitable for children aged 9-10 (3rd-4th grades of elementary school)

Evaluates the ability to comprehend short sentences and conversations related to everyday situations or topics.

BASIC

Suitable for children aged 11-12 (5th–6th grades of elementary school)

Evaluates the ability to communicate about personal information, daily activities, future plans, and past experiences in written and spoken language.

JUNIOR

Suitable for middle school students

Evaluates the ability to comprehend short paragraphs, practical texts, and speech covering general topics and to participate in simple daily conversations.

HIGH JUNIOR

Suitable for high school students

Evaluates the ability to use English fluently, accurately, and effectively on a wide range of social and academic subjects, as well as the ability to use sentences with a variety of complex structures.

ADVANCED

Suitable for university students and adults

Evaluates the ability to use practical English required for a job or work environment, as well as the ability to use and understand English at the university level.

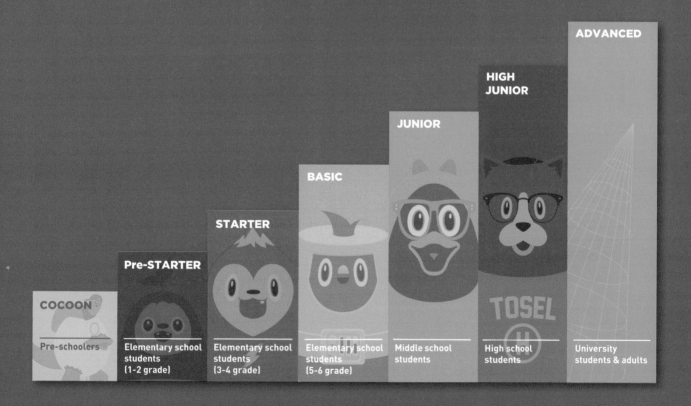

COCOON

Pre-schoolers

Pre-STARTER

Elementary school students (1-2 grade)

STARTER

Elementary school students (3-4 grade)

BASIC

Elementary school students (5-6 grade)

JUNIOR

Middle school students

HIGH JUNIOR

High school students

ADVANCED

University students & adults

Evaluation

Assessing the Four Skills

TOSEL evaluates the four language skills: reading, listening, speaking and writing, through indirect and direct assessment items.

This system of evaluation is part of a concerted effort to break away from materials geared solely toward grammar and reading-oriented education.

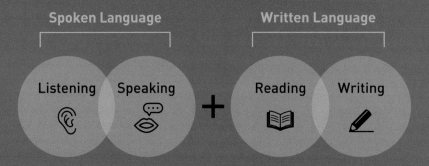

TOSEL Test Information

Level	Score	Grade	Section	
			Section I Listening & Speaking	Section II Reading & Writing
COCOON	100		15 Questions / 15 min	15 Questions / 15 min
Pre-STARTER	100		15 Questions / 15 min	20 Questions / 25 min
STARTER	100		20 Questions / 15 min	20 Questions / 25 min
BASIC	100	1-10	30 Questions / 20 min	30 Questions / 30 min
JUNIOR	100		30 Questions / 20 min	30 Questions / 30 min
HIGH JUNIOR	100		30 Questions / 25 min	35 Questions / 35 min
ADVANCED	990		70 Questions / 45 min	70 Questions / 55 min

Certificates

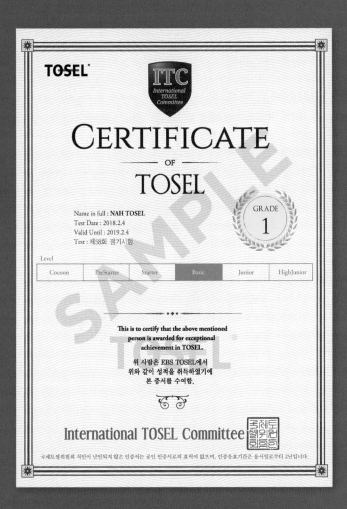

TOSEL Certificate

The International TOSEL Committee officially evaluates and certifies the level of English proficiency of English learners from the age of 4 to adults.

Certified by

Mar. 2010   Korea University

Dec. 2009   The Korean Society of Speech Science

Dec. 2009   The Korea Association of Foreign Language Education

Nov. 2009   The Applied Linguistics Association of Korea

Oct. 2009   The Pan Korea English Teachers Association

CHAPTER 1

Social Studies / Psychology

Teacher's Book
p.184

UNIT 1

Forms of Government

Name three countries that have a monarchy.
Have you ever been to any of those countries?

Governments are political and legal systems that control people's relationships with one another within a society. Over history, humans have developed many types of government. Two of those types are described here.

The first type is monarchy. From ancient times until the early 20th century, this was the most common form of government. In this type of government, a queen or king is the ruler, and power is handed down from parent to child. Currently, there are still monarchies in countries around the world, but they tend to be constitutional monarchies, where most power lies with elected officials instead of with the king or queen. The UK is an example of a constitutional monarchy. Saudi Arabia is an example of an absolute monarchy, where the royal head is the ruler of the state.

Another form of government is democracy, whereby citizens organize political parties and compete in elections for transfer of power. There are two common forms of democracy. In a presidential democracy, a chief is elected and given a lot of power. The power is then limited by the constitution and other legal factors. France and the United States are both presidential democracies. In a parliamentary democracy, such as the one in India or Australia, the country's political power is in the parliament, and the head of the country must be a member of parliament.

New Words

monarchy	ruler
n a form of government with a royal family	*n* a leader

elect	official
v vote for	*n* a public authority

democracy	citizen
n a form of government whereby citizens vote for the leader	*n* a legal member of a state

Part A. Picture Description

 10 minutes

1.

It is time to _____ our new leader.

(A) fire
(B) elect
(C) promote
(D) celebrate

2.

Achara is a German _____.

(A) pilot
(B) citizen
(C) teacher
(D) monarch

Part B. Sentence Completion

3. Kings and queens have ruled since ancient times, and there are _____ some ruling certain countries.

(A) yet
(B) still
(C) not as
(D) already

4. In our team, we have a rule _____ latecomers have to pay a fine.

(A) how
(B) which
(C) whereby
(D) however

You probably already knew that England has a royal family, but did you know these facts about the British monarchy?

1) For a long time, the royal family had no family names. They used only their first names. Then in 1917, King George V decided that males in the family would have the last name "Windsor." Still today, some British princes generally use no family name.

2) Britain's monarch, Queen Elizabeth II has had the longest reign of any British monarch. She took the throne in 1952. That makes her one of the longest reigning monarchs of all time in any country.

3) Every Tuesday, the Queen meets with the UK's prime minister. So far, there have been thirteen prime ministers during the Queen's reign. She also hosts events for international leaders.

5. According to the information, what is true about the British royal family?

(A) They began their reign in 1952.
(B) Until 1917, the family name was "Windsor."
(C) The current queen is named Windsor Elizabeth I.
(D) Some members currently do not use a family name.

6. Which is NOT mentioned about the British monarch?

(A) her weekly meetings with the prime minister
(B) her encounters with non-British world leaders
(C) how she gets to and from Buckingham Palace
(D) how many British prime ministers she has worked with

Part D. General Reading Comprehension

Governments are political and legal systems that control people's relationships with one another within a society. Over history, humans have developed many types of government. Two of those types are described here.

The first type is monarchy. From ancient times until the early 20th century, this was the most common form of government. In this type of government, a queen or king is the ruler, and power is handed down from parent to child. Currently, there are still monarchies in countries around the world, but they tend to be constitutional monarchies, where most power lies with elected officials instead of with the king or queen. The UK is an example of a constitutional monarchy. Saudi Arabia is an example of an absolute monarchy, where the royal head is the ruler of the state.

Another form of government is democracy, whereby citizens organize political parties and compete in elections for transfer of power. There are two common forms of democracy. In a presidential democracy, a chief is elected and given a lot of power. The power is then limited by the constitution and other legal factors. France and the United States are both presidential democracies. In a parliamentary democracy, such as the one in India or Australia, the country's political power is in the parliament, and the head of the country must be a member of parliament.

7. What is the main topic of the passage?

(A) some alternatives to monarchy
(B) two different forms of government
(C) typical changes in government over time
(D) the pros and cons of monarchy or democracy

8. According to the passage, what is true about monarchy?

(A) It did not exist until the 20th century.
(B) It first began in 12th-century England.
(C) It involves power transfer through elections.
(D) It was very common before the 21st century.

9. Which country is listed as an absolute monarchy?

(A) North Korea
(B) Saudi Arabia
(C) the United States
(D) the United Kingdom

10. According to the passage, what is true about parliamentary democracy?

(A) France is an example of such a democracy.
(B) Leaders hand power down to their children.
(C) Citizens are banned from forming political parties.
(D) The country's leader must be a member of parliament.

Listening Practice

 Listen and write.

  MP3 HJ3-1

Forms of Government

Governments are political and legal systems that control people's relationships with one another within a society. Over history, humans have developed many types of government. Two of those types are described here.

The first type is ¹ _____. From ancient times until the early 20th century, this was the most common form of government. In this type of government, a queen or king is the ² _____, and power is handed down from parent to child. Currently, there are still monarchies in countries around the world, but they tend to be constitutional monarchies, where most power lies with elected ³ _____ instead of with the king or queen. The UK is an example of a constitutional monarchy. Saudi Arabia is an example of an absolute monarchy, where the royal head is the ruler of the state.

Another form of government is democracy, whereby ⁴ _____ organize political parties and compete in elections for transfer of power. There are two common forms of democracy. In a presidential democracy, a chief is ⁵ _____ and given a lot of power. The power is then limited by the constitution and other legal factors. France and the United States are both presidential democracies. In a parliamentary ⁶ _____, such as the one in India or Australia, the country's political power is in the parliament, and the head of the country must be a member of parliament.

Word Bank

oficials	luler	monarky
officials	elected	citizens
ruler	citisens	monarchy
erected	democrasy	democracy

 Listen. Pause. Say each sentence.

  MP3 HJ3-1G

Writing Practice

 Write the words.

1 _____ *n* a form of government with a royal family	2 _____ *n* a leader
3 _____ *v* vote for	4 _____ *n* a public authority
5 _____ *n* a form of government whereby citizens vote for the leader	6 _____ *n* a legal member of a state

 Write the words in each blank.

Summary

Two types of government are monarchy and democracy. In a monarchy, a king or queen is the ruler and power is handed down from _____ to child. Most monarchies nowadays are constitutional monarchies. Another form is _____, whereby citizens organize political parties and _____ for someone to hand over power. Two types of this form are presidential democracy and _____ democracy.

Word Puzzle

 Complete the word puzzle.

Across

3 a form of government with a royal family

5 a legal member of a state

6 a leader

Down

1 a form of government whereby citizens vote for the leader

2 vote for

4 a public authority

UNIT 2

 Teacher's Book p.189

A Violinist in the Station

Imagine you are taking the subway to school in the morning.
A musician is playing in the subway station.
Do you stop and listen?

During a January, 2007 Friday morning rush hour in Washington, D.C. a busking violinist played six classical songs over 43 minutes in a subway station. Of the over 1,000 people who passed by, only seven stopped to listen. Twenty-seven people put some money in the busker's open violin case. The earnings totaled $52.17. However, what the commuters did not know was that the musician was the virtuoso violinist Joshua Bell. Unknowingly, the commuters were participating in a social experiment organized by a newspaper.

The experiment's purpose was to raise questions related to beauty and busy city life. One question was whether people could recognize that something was extremely beautiful without being told that it was. The songs that Bell played were carefully selected as classical masterpieces that most people would not recognize. Bell was also dressed in plain clothes instead of a tuxedo. No one introduced him. Still, he played as beautifully as if he had been in a concert hall. Another question was about whether busy city people appreciated beauty as a central part of life. Are people driven too much by money, making too little time for art and beauty?

It is not certain why more people did not stop to listen. Surely, some commuters worried about being late for work. Others may have been cautious around buskers. Still, the low earnings and small number of listeners in the experiment raise interesting questions about beauty and modern life.

New Words

rush hour	commuter
n a busy time for traffic	*n* someone traveling to or from work
earnings	driven by
n money made from work	*adj* motivated by
appreciate	cautious
v respect and admire	*adj* careful

Part A. Picture Description

1.

There are five _____.

(A) drivers
(B) strollers
(C) commuters
(D) pedestrians

2.

In terms of safety, Misha is more _____ than Bill.

(A) dazed
(B) daring
(C) cautious
(D) careless

Part B. Sentence Completion

3. We knew she was a great musician. What we did not know, though, _____ was also a great sculptor.

(A) was that she
(B) she was that
(C) that she was
(D) it was she that

4. Only ten people _____ at Mark's painting yesterday. However, those ten people who stopped and looked said it was beautiful.

(A) stopped to look
(B) stopped looking
(C) have stopped to look
(D) have stopped looking

Learn to Appreciate the Beauty around You!

1. Look for little things all around you can appreciate. Do you see some pretty flowers growing on the side of the road? Stop and take a close look. Is there a piece of art on the wall of the cafe where you're working? Why not get up from your table and check it out in more detail?

2. Put yourself in places where you can have a feeling of awe and inspiration. Getting out into nature is one good place for this. Art, history, and science museums can inspire awe, too, as can live concerts and theater.

3. Take your headphones out when you pass a busker. Sure, there is awe-inspiring music in your headphones. But if you pass a busker, take your headphones out and listen. Otherwise, you could miss the music of a virtuoso violinist like Joshua Bell!

5. Which of the following is a given tip?

   (A) Smell more flowers.
   (B) Go to modern coffee shops.
   (C) Buy paintings for your house.
   (D) Look more closely at beautiful things.

6. According to the passage, what is NOT true about awe?

   (A) Museums rarely provide a sense of awe.
   (B) Live theater in concert halls inspires awe.
   (C) Nature is a good place to experience awe.
   (D) Songs in headphones can remind us of awe.

Part D. General Reading Comprehension

During a January, 2007 Friday morning rush hour in Washington, D.C. a busking violinist played six classical songs over 43 minutes in a subway station. Of the over 1,000 people who passed by, only seven stopped to listen. Twenty-seven people put some money in the busker's open violin case. The earnings totaled $52.17. However, what the commuters did not know was that the musician was the virtuoso violinist Joshua Bell. Unknowingly, the commuters were participating in a social experiment organized by a newspaper.

The experiment's purpose was to raise questions related to beauty and busy city life. One question was whether people could recognize that something was extremely beautiful without being told that it was. The songs that Bell played were carefully selected as classical masterpieces that most people would not recognize. Bell was also dressed in plain clothes instead of a tuxedo. No one introduced him. Still, he played as beautifully as if he had been in a concert hall. Another question was about whether busy city people appreciated beauty as a central part of life. Are people driven too much by money, making too little time for art and beauty?

It is not certain why more people did not stop to listen. Surely, some commuters worried about being late for work. Others may have been cautious around buskers. Still, the low earnings and small number of listeners in the experiment raise interesting questions about beauty and modern life.

---

7. Which sentence best describes the experiment?

   (A) A subway line invited commuters to play instruments.
   (B) A rock star decided to switch to playing classical music.
   (C) A famous violinist pretended to busk in a busy subway station.
   (D) A violinist lost his job and had to work busking in a subway station.

8. Why did the newspaper conduct the experiment?

   (A) to investigate modern city life and beauty
   (B) to see whether subways were getting quieter
   (C) to find out why children dislike classical music
   (D) to learn how much to charge for concert tickets

9. Which of the following is NOT mentioned?

   (A) the clothing Bell wore
   (B) the money Bell earned
   (C) how long Bell played for
   (D) which station Bell played in

10. Which of the following statements about the experiment would its researchers most likely agree with?

   (A) "This proves that subway stations have the best sound systems."
   (B) "This may show that city people are not taking time to appreciate beauty."
   (C) "This likely reveals how commuters prefer listening to musicians in jeans."
   (D) "This demonstrates that musicians' fame does not influence an audience's feelings."

Listening Practice

Listen and write.

  MP3 HJ3-2

A Violinist in the Station

During a January, 2007 Friday morning ¹ _____ in Washington, D.C. a busking violinist played six classical songs over 43 minutes in a subway station. Of the over 1,000 people who passed by, only seven stopped to listen. Twenty-seven people put some money in the busker's open violin case. The ² _____ totaled $52.17. However, what the ³ _____ did not know was that the musician was the virtuoso violinist Joshua Bell. Unknowingly, the commuters were participating in a social experiment organized by a newspaper.

The experiment's purpose was to raise questions related to beauty and busy city life. One question was whether people could recognize that something was extremely beautiful without being told that it was. The songs that Bell played were carefully selected as classical masterpieces that most people would not recognize. Bell was also dressed in plain clothes instead of a tuxedo. No one introduced him. Still, he played as beautifully as if he had been in a concert hall. Another question was about whether busy city people ⁴ _____ beauty as a central part of life. Are people ⁵ _____ too much by money, making too little time for art and beauty?

It is not certain why more people did not stop to listen. Surely, some commuters worried about being late for work. Others may have been ⁶ _____ around buskers. Still, the low earnings and small number of listeners in the experiment raise interesting questions about beauty and modern life.

Word Bank

appreciated	rushour	commuters
driven	comuters	coutious
earnings	cautious	driben
ernings	rush hour	appreciate

 Listen. Pause. Say each sentence.

  MP3 HJ3-2G

Writing Practice

 Write the words.

1 _____

n　a busy time for traffic

2 _____

n　someone traveling to or from work

3 _____

n　money made from work

4 _____

adj　motivated by

5 _____

v　respect and admire

6 _____

adj　careful

 Write the words in each blank.

Summary

Rush-hour commuters were unknowingly participating in a social experiment. A famous _____ pretended to be a _____. He played unfamiliar songs, and only a few people stopped to listen or give him money. The _____ of the research was to explore whether busy city people _____ beauty as a central part of life.

Word Puzzle

 Complete the word puzzle.

Across

2 someone traveling to or from work

4 motivated by

5 careful

6 a busy time for traffic

Down

1 respect and admire

3 money made from work

UNIT 3

Biopiracy: The Neem Tree

Do people own ideas? If so, how can they prove ownership?

When genetics researchers use and copyright local people's traditional ideas about trees and plants without proper permission or acknowledgement, it is called "biopiracy." One prime example of biopiracy is the case of the neem tree.

The neem tree has been used by people in India for thousands of years. Its many uses include toothpastes, pesticides, skin care treatments, and lamp oil. However, in 1995 an American company was able to copyright one property of the neem tree. Indian farmers argued that it was not right for the US company to get a copyright. After all, to get a copyright an inventor must prove that there is no prior existing knowledge of the product. The farmers pointed out that knowledge of the neem tree's special properties had existed for a long time. However, according to European patent law, "prior knowledge" could only be shown if it had been published in a scientific journal, so the copyright office granted a patent to the American company.

There was a legal battle, and ten years later the European Patent Office cancelled the copyright. The court found enough evidence that there was prior knowledge of neem seed properties in traditional Indian farming techniques. Activists and farmers argued that the neem tree case was an example of biopiracy. Since then, activists have asked for laws to be strengthened to defend traditional knowledge in countries around the world.

New Words

copyright	permission
v get legal rights to	*n* approval

pesticide	property
n something used to kill insects on crops	*n* a characteristic

patent	activist
n a licence for an invention	*n* someone campaigning for social change

Part A. Picture Description

1.

There were many _____ at the event.

(A) scarves
(B) activists
(C) antelopes
(D) snorkelers

2.

The farmer uses _____ on his crops.

(A) an ox
(B) a tractor
(C) pesticide
(D) auto-irrigation

Part B. Sentence Completion

3. _____ the new law, you are not allowed to smoke near a bus stop.

(A) According
(B) Accorded
(C) According to
(D) It is accorded

4. Even before this company produced their toothpaste, local people _____ the paste's key ingredients for centuries.

(A) had been used
(B) had been using
(C) have been used
(D) have been using

Heena Anti-Acne Neem Face Wash

Our specially patented formula helps clear up your skin within just 7 days, guaranteed. Use this anti-inflammatory, antiseptic face wash twice a day on moistened skin, avoiding the area around the eyes. Use in conjunction with our patented face moisturizer. Key ingredients: neem, turmeric, tea-tree oil.

Contains 120g

Copyright 2020 Heena Cosmetics.

5. What does the label promise that the product does?

   (A) get rid of skin wrinkles
   (B) help skin near the eyes
   (C) clear acne from problem skin
   (D) moisturize the skin of the knees

6. Which of the following does the label advise?

   (A) using another product as well
   (B) patting the skin around the eyes
   (C) drying the skin carefully after use
   (D) asking a doctor about inflammation

Part D. General Reading Comprehension

When genetics researchers use and copyright local people's traditional ideas about trees and plants without proper permission or acknowledgement, it is called "biopiracy." One prime example of biopiracy is the case of the neem tree.

The neem tree has been used by people in India for thousands of years. Its many uses include toothpastes, pesticides, skin care treatments, and lamp oil. However, in 1995 an American company was able to copyright one property of the neem tree. Indian farmers argued that it was not right for the US company to get a copyright. After all, to get a copyright an inventor must prove that there is no prior existing knowledge of the product. The farmers pointed out that knowledge of the neem tree's special properties had existed for a long time. However, according to European patent law, "prior knowledge" could only be shown if it had been published in a scientific journal, so the copyright office granted a patent to the American company.

There was a legal battle, and ten years later the European Patent Office cancelled the copyright. The court found enough evidence that there was prior knowledge of neem seed properties in traditional Indian farming techniques. Activists and farmers argued that the neem tree case was an example of biopiracy. Since then, activists have asked for laws to be strengthened to defend traditional knowledge in countries around the world.

7. What would be the best title for the passage?

(A) Tree Science: Legal Definitions
(B) Biopiracy: The Neem Tree Case
(C) Genetically Engineering a Tree
(D) Biology and India's Sacred Tree

8. What use of the neem tree is NOT listed?

(A) lamp oil
(B) pesticide
(C) toothpaste
(D) shoe polish

9. According to the passage, why did European patent law overrule Indian farmers in 1995?

(A) Their farms were already very successful.
(B) Their knowledge had been proven as faulty.
(C) The neem tree could be found in many countries.
(D) The traditional knowledge was not in a scientific journal.

10. According to the passage, what has happened since the neem seed case?

(A) Activists have cut down foreign trees.
(B) Some farmers have burnt down court buildings.
(C) Activists have started planting neem seeds in every country.
(D) Some people want legal changes to defend traditional knowledge.

Listen and write.

  MP3 HJ3-3

Biopiracy: The Neem Tree

When genetics researchers use and __¹_____ local people's traditional ideas about trees and plants without proper __²_____ or acknowledgement, it is called "biopiracy." One prime example of biopiracy is the case of the neem tree.

The neem tree has been used by people in India for thousands of years. Its many uses include toothpastes, __³_____, skin care treatments, and lamp oil. However, in 1995 an American company was able to copyright one __⁴_____ of the neem tree. Indian farmers argued that it was not right for the US company to get a copyright. After all, to get a copyright an inventor must prove that there is no prior existing knowledge of the product. The farmers pointed out that knowledge of the neem tree's special properties had existed for a long time. However, according to European __⁵_____ law, "prior knowledge" could only be shown if it had been published in a scientific journal, so the copyright office granted a patent to the American company.

There was a legal battle, and ten years later the European Patent Office cancelled the copyright. The court found enough evidence that there was prior knowledge of neem seed properties in traditional Indian farming techniques. __⁶_____ and farmers argued that the neem tree case was an example of biopiracy. Since then, activists have asked for laws to be strengthened to defend traditional knowledge in countries around the world.

Word Bank

pesticides	permision	permission
propurty	property	copywrite
Activists	festicies	patent
petent	Activist	copyright

 Listen. Pause. Say each sentence.

  MP3 HJ3-3G

Writing Practice

 Write the words.

1 _____

 v get legal rights to

2 _____

 n approval

3 _____

 n something used to kill insects on crops

4 _____

 n a characteristic

5 _____

 n a licence for an invention

6 _____

 n someone campaigning for social change

 Write the words in each blank.

Summary

Biopiracy is when researchers copyright _____ knowledge. The case of the neem tree is a well-known example. The neem tree has been used by people in _____ for thousands of years. But an American company tried to patent its _____. After a long legal _____, the patent was cancelled.

Word Puzzle

 Complete the word puzzle.

Across

1 approval

4 get legal rights to

5 a licence for an invention

Down

1 something used to kill insects on crops

2 a characteristic

3 someone campaigning for social change

UNIT 4

A Hierarchy of Needs

Teacher's Book
p.201

What do you think people need the most in life?

Maslow's Hierarchy of Needs is a popular psychology model proposed by Abraham Maslow in 1943 to explain what motivates human beings. The model ranks five things people require in life. At the first level are basic physical needs, including things like food and water. These are followed in order by safety needs, the need for social belonging, self-esteem, and "self-actualization" (the need to fill one's potential in life).

Despite its popular use, Maslow's Hierarchy has numerous criticisms. One major criticism relates to the methodology of Maslow's research. Maslow observed people, but his research did not involve experiments and he did not clearly define the terms he used. That means his claims cannot be properly tested.

Moreover, Maslow studied very few people. Importantly, he refused to observe people with mental or physical disabilities. Also, societies differ. Some societies value individual needs more whereas some value group needs more. In addition, it has been found that people prioritize their needs differently at different ages and moments in life. What's more, Maslow himself recognized that individuals differed when it came to needs; as a result, it is not clear how useful the theory could be.

In short, Maslow's Hierarchy of Needs model is lacking as a theory. It is hoped that more research in such fields as psychology and biology can help us to understand human motivation better.

New Words

psychology	**motivate**
n the scientific study of the mind	*v* inspire
self-esteem	**claim**
n respect for yourself	*n* an argument that something is true
belonging	**prioritize**
n feeling that you are in the right place	*v* put in order of most important

Part A. Picture Description

1.

Having a holiday meal together gives the Smiths a sense of _____.

(A) shame
(B) confusion
(C) belonging
(D) disappointment

2.

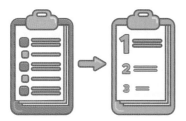

I _____ today's tasks. I made a to-do list.

(A) criticized
(B) prioritized
(C) visualized
(D) randomized

Part B. Sentence Completion

3.   Despite _____, this idea has a few problems.

(A) it's popular
(B) it is popular
(C) its popularity
(D) it's popularity

4.   Not only did others criticize Dad's idea, but Dad _____ even doubted whether it was a good plan.

(A) he
(B) his
(C) him
(D) himself

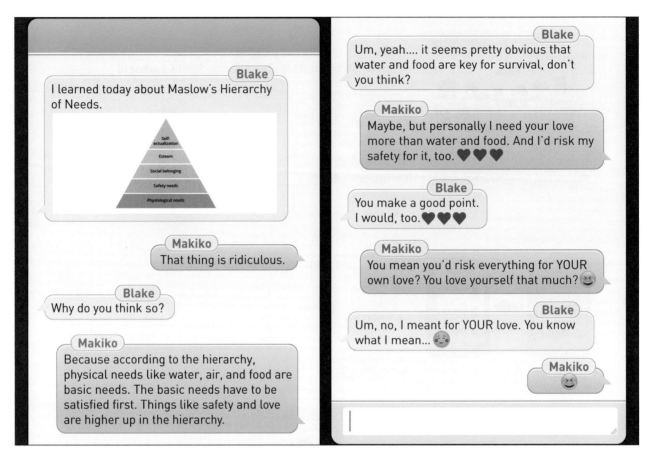

5. What does Blake say about Maslow's Hierarchy of Needs?

    (A) that he taught a class on it
    (B) that he just learned about it
    (C) that he feels it is bad science
    (D) that he studied it the year before

6. What does Makiko mean when she says, "I'd risk my safety for it"?

    (A) She thinks Blake should enjoy life more.
    (B) She used to love doing an extreme sport.
    (C) She is willing to face danger for Blake's love.
    (D) She thinks safety matters more than water and food.

Part D. General Reading Comprehension

Maslow's Hierarchy of Needs is a popular psychology model proposed by Abraham Maslow in 1943 to explain what motivates human beings. The model ranks five things people require in life. At the first level are basic physical needs, including things like food and water. These are followed in order by safety needs, the need for social belonging, self-esteem, and "self-actualization" (the need to fill one's potential in life).

Despite its popular use, Maslow's Hierarchy has numerous criticisms. One major criticism relates to the methodology of Maslow's research. Maslow observed people, but his research did not involve experiments and he did not clearly define the terms he used. That means his claims cannot be properly tested.

Moreover, Maslow studied very few people. Importantly, he refused to observe people with mental or physical disabilities. Also, societies differ. Some societies value individual needs more whereas some value group needs more. In addition, it has been found that people prioritize their needs differently at different ages and moments in life. What's more, Maslow himself recognized that individuals differed when it came to needs; as a result, it is not clear how useful the theory could be.

In short, Maslow's Hierarchy of Needs model is lacking as a theory. It is hoped that more research in such fields as psychology and biology can help us to understand human motivation better.

7. What is the passage mainly about?

   (A) the life and times of a psychologist
   (B) a motivation model that ranks human needs
   (C) differences between human and animal needs
   (D) changes in psychology theory in the 20th century

8. What is NOT mentioned about methodology?

   (A) keeping mice
   (B) defining terms
   (C) observing people
   (D) conducting experiments

9. What does the passage say about age?

   (A) People value society more when they are older.
   (B) People tend to have physical problems later in life.
   (C) People think like individuals when they are teenagers.
   (D) People have different priorities at different stages in life.

10. Which of the following best describes the tone of the passage in relation to Maslow's Hierarchy of Needs?

   (A) critical
   (B) neutral
   (C) intimidated
   (D) appreciative

Listen and write.

  MP3 HJ3-4

A Hierarchy of Needs

Maslow's Hierarchy of Needs is a popular [1]_____ model proposed by Abraham Maslow in 1943 to explain what [2]_____ human beings. The model ranks five things people require in life. At the first level are basic physical needs, including things like food and water. These are followed in order by safety needs, the need for social [3]_____, [4]_____, and "self-actualization" (the need to fill one's potential in life).

Despite its popular use, Maslow's Hierarchy has numerous criticisms. One major criticism relates to the methodology of Maslow's research. Maslow observed people, but his research did not involve experiments and he did not clearly define the terms he used. That means his [5]_____ cannot be properly tested.

Moreover, Maslow studied very few people. Importantly, he refused to observe people with mental or physical disabilities. Also, societies differ. Some societies value individual needs more whereas some value group needs more. In addition, it has been found that people [6]_____ their needs differently at different ages and moments in life. What's more, Maslow himself recognized that individuals differed when it came to needs; as a result, it is not clear how useful the theory could be.

In short, Maslow's Hierarchy of Needs model is lacking as a theory. It is hoped that more research in such fields as psychology and biology can help us to understand human motivation better.

Word Bank

motivates	clames	prioritize
self-esteem	proiritize	motivate
psychology	psycology	self-estim
belounging	belonging	claims

 Listen. Pause. Say each sentence.

  MP3 HJ3-4G

Writing Practice

 Write the words.

1 _____	2 _____
n the scientific study of the mind	*v* inspire

3 _____	4 _____
n respect for yourself	*n* an argument that something is true

5 _____	6 _____
n feeling that you are in the right place	*v* put in order of most important

 Write the words in each blank.

Summary

Maslow's _____ of Needs ranks five things people require in life. However, despite its _____ use, the model has numerous criticisms. It is hoped that more research in such fields as psychology and _____ can help us to understand human _____ better.

Word Puzzle

Complete the word puzzle.

Across

4 put in order of most important

5 inspire

Down

1 respect for yourself

2 an argument that something is true

3 feeling that you are in the right place

4 the scientific study of the mind

The Mysterious Cruelty of Henry the Eighth

Teacher's Book p.208

Henry the Eighth, the king of England from 1509 to 1547, was an infamously cruel monarch. He divorced two of his six wives and had two others killed. He also had many of his closest friends and advisors killed. However, when he was still a young man, he had been known for having a much more reasonable personality. So what went wrong?

It is entirely possible that Henry the Eighth's cruelty simply stemmed from his having absolute power. However, he had had absolute power in his earlier years as king, as well, and had not been so irrational. Therefore, some psychologists and historians believe that the king's cruel impulses started after he suffered from an injury to the head.

In the 1600s, jousting was a popular activity among royals and other rich people. This violent sport involved attacking an opponent with a weapon while wearing armor on horseback. In 1524, Henry the Eighth suffered several hard blows to the head during jousting tournaments. In one tournament, a horse fell on him. After that point, people started describing him as angry and violent. At the time, people would not have known about the link between head injuries and violent impulses.

Was Henry the Eighth's cruelty a result of the head injury? Or was he simply an irrational absolute monarch? It is one of the mysteries of history.

CHAPTER 2

Culture

UNIT 5

Mythical Creatures

Draw a picture of a mythical creature from your country.
Then describe what you've drawn.

UNIT 5 Mythical Creatures

Cultures all over the world have developed folklore about mythological creatures. Interestingly, many of these fantastical beasts are human-animal hybrids.

Horse-human hybrids are one common example. *Centaurs*, for example, have the bottom and legs of a horse but the upper body and head of a human. *Satyrs*, ancient Greek nature spirits, have the body of a male human but the ears and tail of a horse.

Another type is the human-bird hybrid. Indian mythology has the *kinnara*, a half-human, half-bird creature. Korean folklore features the *inmyeonjo*, which has a bird body and human face.

There are also many human-fish hybrids. Most famous of these, perhaps, are *mermaids* and *mermen*, who are human from the waist up, but have a long fish tail. These creatures have variations. In the mythology of some Philippine islands, for example, *magindara* are vicious mermaids with sharp scales who sometimes save and sometimes attack fishermen.

Some hybrids also include parts of multiple beasts. For instance, the Russian *meduza* has the head of a woman, body of a beast, the mouth of a snake, the legs of an elephant, and the tail of a dragon. The early Persian *manticore* has the head of a human, the body of a lion, and a spiny, venomous tail.

Cultures change over time and across regions. However, a common link among the world's people is a fascination with mythological human-animal hybrid creatures.

New Words

folklore	beast
n traditional stories of a culture	*n* an animal
mythological	hybrid
adj relating to myths or fables	*n* something made by combining two other things
vicious	scales
adj cruel	*n* the overlapping plates on the skin of reptiles

Part A. Picture Description

1.

It is a _____ of a lion and a bird.

(A) cage
(B) hybrid
(C) legend
(D) photograph

2.

That dog is _____.

(A) vicious
(B) friendly
(C) sleeping
(D) benevolent

Part B. Sentence Completion

3. A common connection among the world's people _____ fascination with fantasy creatures.

(A) is a
(B) are a
(C) is these
(D) are these

4. This fantasy creature is a type of fish _____ large fangs.

(A) has
(B) with
(C) have
(D) with having

Video game

Beast Slayer

Key Characters: Minotaur, Theseus, Ariadne

Story background:

In Greek mythology, the Minotaur was a ferocious monster with the body of a man and the head and tail of a bull. It was shut away by King Minos in the Labyrinth, a giant maze. One day, King Minos's son was killed in battle by Athenians. In revenge, King Minos decided that fourteen young Athenians would be sent every year to be eaten by the Minotaur. The third time this happened, the young Athenian hero Theseus volunteered to be sent to the Minotaur, promising to end the beast's life. He felt confident he could do it, but the problem was getting out of the Labyrinth. To help him, Minos's daughter Ariadne gave Theseus a ball of thread. Theseus laid the thread down in the maze to help him find his way out again. He killed the Minotaur, and he and Ariadne escaped to Athens. In this video game, the story of Theseus and Ariadne continues...

5.   Who killed the Minotaur?

(A) an old king
(B) a young Athenian
(C) the son of King Minos
(D) the brother of Ariadne

6.   How did Theseus escape the Labyrinth?

(A) by sailing on his shield
(B) by crawling up the walls
(C) by following some thread
(D) by making a trail of breadcrumbs

Part D. General Reading Comprehension

Cultures all over the world have developed folklore about mythological creatures. Interestingly, many of these fantastical beasts are human-animal hybrids.

Horse-human hybrids are one common example. *Centaurs*, for example, have the bottom and legs of a horse but the upper body and head of a human. *Satyrs*, ancient Greek nature spirits, have the body of a male human but the ears and tail of a horse.

Another type is the human-bird hybrid. Indian mythology has the *kinnara*, a half-human, half-bird creature. Korean folklore features the *inmyeonjo*, which has a bird body and human face.

There are also many human-fish hybrids. Most famous of these, perhaps, are *mermaids* and *mermen*, who are human from the waist up, but have a long fish tail. These creatures have variations. In the mythology of some Philippine islands, for example, *magindara* are vicious mermaids with sharp scales who sometimes save and sometimes attack fishermen.

Some hybrids also include parts of multiple beasts. For instance, the Russian *meduza* has the head of a woman, body of a beast, the mouth of a snake, the legs of an elephant, and the tail of a dragon. The early Persian *manticore* has the head of a human, the body of a lion, and a spiny, venomous tail.

Cultures change over time and across regions. However, a common link among the world's people is a fascination with mythological human-animal hybrid creatures.

7. What would be the best title for the passage?

(A) Animals in Cultures around the World
(B) Myths and Facts about Common Pets
(C) Part Human, Part Animal: Mythology Hybrids
(D) Hybrid Animals of the Future: The Role of Genetics

8. Which Greek spirit looks like a man with a horse's tail and ears?

(A) the satyr
(B) the unicorn
(C) the centaur
(D) the manticore

9. According to the passage, how are the *kinnara* and *inmyeonjo* similar?

(A) They both are hybrids of fish.
(B) They both make the sound of a lion.
(C) They both come from Indian mythology.
(D) They both have human and bird features.

10. What is true about the *meduza*?

(A) It has the legs of a lion.
(B) It is from the Philippines.
(C) Its head is like a dragon's.
(D) Its mouth is like a snake's.

Listening Practice

 Listen and write.

  MP3 HJ3-5

Mythical Creatures

Cultures all over the world have developed ¹ _____ about ² _____ creatures. Interestingly, many of these fantastical ³ _____ are human-animal hybrids.

Horse-human hybrids are one common example. *Centaurs*, for example, have the bottom and legs of a horse but the upper body and head of a human. *Satyrs*, ancient Greek nature spirits, have the body of a male human but the ears and tail of a horse.

Another type is the human-bird hybrid. Indian mythology has the *kinnara*, a half-human, half-bird creature. Korean folklore features the *inmyeonjo*, which has a bird body and human face.

There are also many human-fish ⁴ _____ . Most famous of these, perhaps, are *mermaids* and *mermen*, who are human from the waist up, but have a long fish tail. These creatures have variations. In the mythology of some Philippine islands, for example, *magindara* are ⁵ _____ mermaids with sharp ⁶ _____ who sometimes save and sometimes attack fishermen.

Some hybrids also include parts of multiple beasts. For instance, the Russian *meduza* has the head of a woman, body of a beast, the mouth of a snake, the legs of an elephant, and the tail of a dragon. The early Persian *manticore* has the head of a human, the body of a lion, and a spiny, venomous tail.

Cultures change over time and across regions. However, a common link among the world's people is a fascination with mythological human-animal hybrid creatures.

Word Bank

mythological	hybrid	hybrids
scales	mythelogical	foklore
beast	skales	beasts
viscous	folklore	vicious

 Listen. Pause. Say each sentence.

  MP3 HJ3-5G

Writing Practice

 Write the words.

1 _____

  n traditional stories of a culture

2 _____

  n an animal

3 _____

  adj relating to myths or fables

4 _____

  n something made by combining two other things

5 _____

  adj cruel

6 _____

  n the overlapping plates on the skin of reptiles

 Write the words in each blank.

Summary

Cultures all over the world have developed folklore about _____ creatures. Many of these fantastical beasts are human-animal _____. Horse-human hybrids are one common example. There are also the human-bird hybrids, human-fish hybrids, and even hybrids including parts of multiple _____. Mythological human-animal hybrid creature is a fascinating culture as a common _____ among the world's people.

Word Puzzle

 Complete the word puzzle.

Across

5 relating to myths or fables

6 an animal

Down

1 cruel

2 something made by combining two other things

3 traditional stories of a culture

4 the overlapping plates on the skin of reptiles

UNIT 6

 Teacher's Book p.214

Ramadan: The Fast

Sometimes people go for a whole day without eating.
What are some reasons they might do that?

Most of the world's 1.6 billion Muslims observe Ramadan each year. Ramadan is the holiest month in the religion of Islam. There are many important rituals during the month, but perhaps one of the most well known elements is the fast.

To fast means not to eat or drink during a set amount of time. For Muslims observing Ramadan, the fasting time is from dawn to dusk. To prepare to fast, people commonly eat a power meal before dawn called the *suhoor*. Then, when it is time to break the fast at dusk, it is common to take a sip of water and eat some dates. There are prayers at sunset, and then family and friends generally join in a huge feast called *iftar*. In places all over the world, Muslim organizations also set up big public tables for a free feast. In many Arab countries, civil servants finish work hours a little earlier during Ramadan to match sundown. In some countries, it is against the law even for non-Muslims to eat in public during daylight hours during Ramadan.

At the end of Ramadan, people mark the breaking of the fast period with three days of religious rituals, prayers, and celebrations. This period is called Eid al-Fitr. During this time, people typically gather with loved ones to exchange gifts and enjoy time together. They think back on Ramadan and look forward to the year ahead.

New Words

holy	**ritual**
adj sacred	*n* an important ceremony, often for a religion
fast	**dusk**
n a period of not eating	*n* the period after sunset
sip of	**loved ones**
n a small drink of	*n* family and friends

Part A. Picture Description

1.

He is having a _____ of tea.

(A) sip
(B) gulp
(C) glass
(D) slurp

2.

We had to hurry home as it was almost _____.

(A) dusk
(B) dawn
(C) daylight
(D) daybreak

Part B. Sentence Completion

3. One _____ well known Islamic months is called Ramadan.

(A) most
(B) the most
(C) of the most
(D) the most of

4. People have gathered with _____ to celebrate.

(A) love one
(B) loved one
(C) loved ones
(D) loved them ones

UNIT 6   Ramadan: The Fast

Moroccan-style stuffed dates are a great treat to break the fast for *iftar* during Ramadan.

Ingredients

- 500g dates
- 140g almonds
- 60g sugar
- 1 1/2 tablespoons orange-flower water
- 1 tablespoon butter, melted
- 1/4 teaspoon cinnamon

Optional

- food coloring
- walnut pieces (for decoration)

Steps

1. Boil some water in a small pot. Add the almonds and boil for two minutes.

2. Make the almond paste. Blend the almonds, sugar, and cinnamon in a blender. Add the butter and orange-flower water. Blend into a paste. You can add food coloring here.

3. Stuff the dates. Option: decorate them with walnuts.

Keep the stuffed dates in an airtight container in the refrigerator.

5. According to the recipe, which is NOT required?

(A) adding nuts as a garnish
(B) putting a filling in some dates
(C) boiling almonds for two minutes
(D) using a blender to make a paste

6. Which of the following is part of the recipe?

(A) a deep freezer
(B) a dash of spice
(C) a storage container
(D) a spoonful of orange juice

Part D. General Reading Comprehension

Most of the world's 1.6 billion Muslims observe Ramadan each year. Ramadan is the holiest month in the religion of Islam. There are many important rituals during the month, but perhaps one of the most well known elements is the fast.

To fast means not to eat or drink during a set amount of time. For Muslims observing Ramadan, the fasting time is from dawn to dusk. To prepare to fast, people commonly eat a power meal before dawn called the *suhoor*. Then, when it is time to break the fast at dusk, it is common to take a sip of water and eat some dates. There are prayers at sunset, and then family and friends generally join in a huge feast called *iftar*. In places all over the world, Muslim organizations also set up big public tables for a free feast. In many Arab countries, civil servants finish work hours a little earlier during Ramadan to match sundown. In some countries, it is against the law even for non-Muslims to eat in public during daylight hours during Ramadan.

At the end of Ramadan, people mark the breaking of the fast period with three days of religious rituals, prayers, and celebrations. This period is called Eid al-Fitr. During this time, people typically gather with loved ones to exchange gifts and enjoy time together. They think back on Ramadan and look forward to the year ahead.

7. What is the main topic of the passage?

(A) the history of Ramadan
(B) the five main holidays in Islam
(C) an important ritual during Ramadan
(D) where most of the world's Muslims live

8. According to the passage, what is "*suhoor*"?

(A) a place to say prayers
(B) a piece of clothing for Ramadan
(C) a large meal eaten before sunrise
(D) a sip of water and dates at sunset

9. Which of the following does the passage mention?

(A) At the end of Ramadan, a prayer called *taheer* is said.
(B) Internationally, there are free public feasts during Ramadan.
(C) In many countries, lentil dumplings are popular during Ramadan.
(D) In Egypt, many people put up lights of tin and glass during Ramadan.

10. What are the days of festivities at the end of Ramadan called?

(A) *iftar*
(B) dusk
(C) *suhoor*
(D) Eid al-Fitr

Listening Practice

 Listen and write.

  MP3 HJ3-6

Ramadan: The Fast

Most of the world's 1.6 billion Muslims observe Ramadan each year. Ramadan is

the ¹ _____ month in the religion of Islam. There are many important

² _____ during the month, but perhaps one of the most well known elements is

the ³ _____ .

To fast means not to eat or drink during a set amount of time. For Muslims observing Ramadan,

the fasting time is from dawn to ⁴ _____ . To prepare to fast, people commonly

eat a power meal before dawn called the *suhoor*. Then, when it is time to break the fast at dusk,

it is common to take a ⁵ _____ of water and eat some dates. There are prayers at

sunset, and then family and friends generally join in a huge feast called *iftar*. In places all over

the world, Muslim organizations also set up big public tables for a free feast. In many Arab

countries, civil servants finish work hours a little earlier during Ramadan to match sundown. In

some countries, it is against the law even for non-Muslims to eat in public during daylight hours

during Ramadan.

At the end of Ramadan, people mark the breaking of the fast period with three days of religious

rituals, prayers, and celebrations. This period is called Eid al-Fitr. During this time, people

typically gather with ⁶ _____ ones to exchange gifts and enjoy time together. They

think back on Ramadan and look forward to the year ahead.

Word Bank

dusc	holyest	loved
fast	dusk	holiest
love	ritual	sip
rituals	past	sips

 Listen. Pause. Say each sentence.

  MP3 HJ3-6G

Writing Practice

 Write the words.

1 _____

adj sacred

2 _____

n an important ceremony, often for a religion

3 _____

n a period of not eating

4 _____

n the period after sunset

5 _____

n a small drink of

6 _____

n family and friends

 Write the words in each blank.

Summary

Ramadan is the holiest month in the _____ of Islam. One of the most well-known _____ is the fast. People do not eat or drink during the fasting time. They prepare to _____ by eating a meal called the *suhoor*. After prayers, family and friends join in a feast called *iftar*. At the end of Ramadan, people mark the breaking of the fast period with _____ days of religious rituals, prayers, and celebrations during Eid al-Fitr.

Word Puzzle

 Complete the word puzzle.

Across

1 sacred

3 the period after sunset

4 a small drink of

6 an important ceremony, often for a religion

Down

2 family and friends

5 a period of not eating

UNIT 7

The Bibliomotocarro

Teacher's Book
p.220

How do you get books to read?

In the southern Italian region of Basilicata, village children come running down the street with delight when they hear a certain truck that plays music. It may seem like the truck in question would be an ice cream truck. However, it is in fact the Bibliomotocarro, a library on wheels.

The population in many Italian villages is aging year by year. The small population of children means that kids may not have easy access to a children's library. In 2003, a retired schoolteacher thought that the children in the villages would have better lives and could develop a love of reading if only they had access to books. He modified a motorcycle, put a portable library on top of it, and loaded it up with 700 children's books. He started driving from village to village with it and has been doing that since 2003. He stops in eight villages with a total journey between them all of 500 kilometers.

Back in 2003, the Internet was not very developed, and Internet connections were slow, so it is understandable that paper books were so popular with kids. However, all these years later, the Bibliomotocarro is still a huge success. It seems that even with electronic alternatives, there may be something special about books we can touch. And, of course, a book can be even more special if it comes hand-delivered in a musical truck.

New Words

delight	population
n happiness	*n* the people living in a place

portable	access to
adj mobile	*n* the opportunity to get close to

load X up with	alternative
v put a lot of items on X	*n* another possibility

Part A. Picture Description

1.

The cooler is _____.

(A) open
(B) burnt
(C) portable
(D) aquamarine

2.

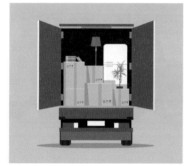

We've already _____ the truck.

(A) emptied
(B) unloaded
(C) loaded up
(D) taken apart

Part B. Sentence Completion

3. The population in that country is aging year _____ year.

(A) in
(B) or
(C) by
(D) as

4. People in remote areas _____ access to cheap food.

(A) may not have
(B) maybe not have
(C) may not be have
(D) maybe not will have

Mobile Library Schedule: October

Date	Village
3	Senose
10	Montamurro
11	Maglionico
12	Monopolli
13	Terranova del Pollo
14	Gorgiglione
17	Venusa
19	Companio

Come enjoy our mobile library. Borrowing books is free. We come by each village 8 times during the school year. Also, come and join our latest projects. In one, children can write stories together. In another, children make short films based on stories they have read.

5. What is true about the mobile library?

(A) It drops by Companio before going to Venusa.
(B) It visits Monopolli immediately after Montamurro.
(C) It is in Maglionico two days before it is in Gorgiglione.
(D) It goes to Terranova del Pollo right after it is in Monopolli.

6. Which activity is NOT offered by the mobile library?

(A) borrowing books
(B) writing stories
(C) creating movies
(D) meeting authors

In the southern Italian region of Basilicata, village children come running down the street with delight when they hear a certain truck that plays music. It may seem like the truck in question would be an ice cream truck. However, it is in fact the Bibliomotocarro, a library on wheels.

The population in many Italian villages is aging year by year. The small population of children means that kids may not have easy access to a children's library. In 2003, a retired schoolteacher thought that the children in the villages would have better lives and could develop a love of reading if only they had access to books. He modified a motorcycle, put a portable library on top of it, and loaded it up with 700 children's books. He started driving from village to village with it and has been doing that since 2003. He stops in eight villages with a total journey between them all of 500 kilometers.

Back in 2003, the Internet was not very developed, and Internet connections were slow, so it is understandable that paper books were so popular with kids. However, all these years later, the Bibliomotocarro is still a huge success. It seems that even with electronic alternatives, there may be something special about books we can touch. And, of course, a book can be even more special if it comes hand-delivered in a musical truck.

7. What would be the best title for the passage?

(A) The Mobile Library of Italy
(B) Nutrition in an Italian School
(C) Ice Cream versus Italian Gelato
(D) How Italian Cars Rule the World

8. Who made the Bibliomotocarro?

(A) a village mayor
(B) a child psychologist
(C) a teenaged engineer
(D) a retired schoolteacher

9. According to the passage, what is true about the Bibliomotocarro?

(A) It began in 2003.
(B) It stops at eighteen villages.
(C) It is made from a modified bicycle.
(D) It can carry a maximum of 70 books.

10. Which statement best matches the passage's conclusion?

(A) "Kids these days still like paper books."
(B) "Kids these days prefer electronics to books."
(C) "Modern children have lost their musical talent."
(D) "Modern children spend too little time outdoors."

Listen and write.

  MP3 HJ3-7

The Bibliomotocarro

In the southern Italian region of Basilicata, village children come running down the street with
_____ when they hear a certain truck that plays music. It may seem like the
truck in question would be an ice cream truck. However, it is in fact the Bibliomotocarro, a
library on wheels.

The 2 _____ in many Italian villages is aging year by year. The small population
of children means that kids may not have easy 3 _____ to a children's library. In
2003, a retired schoolteacher thought that the children in the villages would have better lives
and could develop a love of reading if only they had access to books. He modified a motorcycle,
put a 4 _____ library on top of it, and 5 _____ with 700 children's
books. He started driving from village to village with it and has been doing that since 2003. He
stops in eight villages with a total journey between them all of 500 kilometers.

Back in 2003, the Internet was not very developed, and Internet connections were slow, so it is
understandable that paper books were so popular with kids. However, all these years later, the
Bibliomotocarro is still a huge success. It seems that even with electronic 6 _____,
there may be something special about books we can touch. And, of course, a book can be even
more special if it comes hand-delivered in a musical truck.

Word Bank

delight	portable	loaded it up
access	pofulation	alternatives
alternetives	acess	population
delite	porteble	load it'd up

 Listen. Pause. Say each sentence.

  MP3 HJ3-7G

Writing Practice

 Write the words.

1 _____

  n happiness

2 _____

  n the people living in a place

3 _____

  adj mobile

4 _____

  n the opportunity to get close to

5 _____ X up with

  v put a lot of items on X

6 _____

  n another possibility

 Write the words in each blank.

Summary

In one Italian region, the _____ of children was so small that they could not easily access a children's library. So a _____ schoolteacher _____ a motorcycle into a library and started to drive it from village to village. Even with electronic _____ nowadays, the modified motorcycle, or "Bibliomotocarro," is still a huge success.

Word Puzzle

 Complete the word puzzle.

Across

2 another possibility

3 the people living in a place

6 mobile

Down

1 happiness

4 the opportunity to get close to

5 put a lot of items on X

Teacher's Book
p.225

UNIT 8

Garífuna Punta

Think of a dance you know how to do.
Explain the steps to someone else.
It's best if you can get up and show it, too!

Visitors to the coasts of Central America may find their feet moving to a beautifully entrancing beat. The music and accompanying dance are called "punta," and they are a part of the special heritage of the Garífuna people.

The Garífuna developed punta music as a way to express their struggles and endurance over time. These days, traditional punta can be heard at parties and celebrations. It is even a part of wakes, a kind of funeral celebration.

Key to punta are two drums made from hollowed out wood covered by the skin of a deer, sheep, or wild pig. These drums create the rousing rhythm, with each drum playing a different beat. Other instruments include shakers and shells. There is also singing, with lyrics traditionally in the Garífuna language.

To dance punta, people move their feet and hips without moving their upper body. They make very small movements of their feet on the ground. They shuffle forward and back while keeping the feet flat, which shakes the knees, hips, and backside. The arms and hands may be lifted up going forward and placed down for backward movements.

In the past few decades, a new fusion form of punta has developed, called punta rock. It involves more instruments, and the lyrics may be in Spanish. However, traditional punta is still very much a part of Garífuna culture.

New Words

coast	accompanying
n land that touches the ocean	*adj* going along with
funeral	hollowed out
n a ceremony when someone dies	*adj* made empty in the middle
rousing	shuffle
adj inspiring	*v* walk with dragging feet

Part A. Picture Description

1.

This bowl is made from a single _____ piece of wood.

(A) leafy
(B) pointy
(C) filled up
(D) hollowed out

2.

Tina the Turtle is _____ his feet.

(A) soaring
(B) shuffling
(C) skipping
(D) slithering

Part B. Sentence Completion

3. Key to this dance _____ the accompanying drums.

(A) is
(B) are
(C) has
(D) have

4. This music can often _____ at traditional celebrations.

(A) hear
(B) we hear
(C) of heard
(D) be heard

How to Dance to Punta Rock

Step 1   You'll need some fast-paced punta rock. You can't go wrong with the music of Donny Principe, but the Punta Fighters, the Garífuna Moderna, Banda Azul are other great options.

Step 2   Get ready to be completely exhausted. Also, at first it could be a bit embarrassing. This dance is not for <u>the faint of heart</u>!

Step 3   It's time to start dancing. You can move your shoulders and arms a bit, but the place with the most motion is the backside, people!

Step 4   Keep that backside moving. Dance in place with just a few spins here and there.

Step 5   You're probably completely exhausted by now. It's time to stop! Congratulations on a job well done.

5.   Which is a recommended band?

(A) Donny Punta
(B) Azul Fighters
(C) Banda Principe
(D) Garífuna Moderna

6.   The underlined "the faint of heart" is closest in meaning to:

(A) those who are old
(B) those who are young
(C) those without courage
(D) those who have never loved

Part D. General Reading Comprehension

Visitors to the coasts of Central America may find their feet moving to a beautifully entrancing beat. The music and accompanying dance are called "punta," and they are a part of the special heritage of the Garífuna people.

The Garífuna developed punta music as a way to express their struggles and endurance over time. These days, traditional punta can be heard at parties and celebrations. It is even a part of wakes, a kind of funeral celebration.

Key to punta are two drums made from hollowed out wood covered by the skin of a deer, sheep, or wild pig. These drums create the rousing rhythm, with each drum playing a different beat. Other instruments include shakers and shells. There is also singing, with lyrics traditionally in the Garífuna language.

To dance punta, people move their feet and hips without moving their upper body. They make very small movements of their feet on the ground. They shuffle forward and back while keeping the feet flat, which shakes the knees, hips, and backside. The arms and hands may be lifted up going forward and placed down for backward movements.

In the past few decades, a new fusion form of punta has developed, called punta rock. It involves more instruments, and the lyrics may be in Spanish. However, traditional punta is still very much a part of Garífuna culture.

7. What is the passage mainly about?

   (A) a toe and ankle bracelet
   (B) a type of music and dance
   (C) a holiday in Central America
   (D) a coastal city called Garífuna

8. According to the passage, which of the following is used to cover the drums?

   (A) deer horns
   (B) sheep wool
   (C) wild pig skin
   (D) abalone shell

9. Which of the following is involved in punta?

   (A) kicking the feet high in the air
   (B) keeping the upper body straight
   (C) shaking the head from left to right
   (D) swinging the legs while seated in a chair

10. According to the passage, which of the following does punta rock include?

   (A) fewer singers
   (B) no instruments
   (C) lyrics in Spanish
   (D) sticks for dancers

Listening Practice

Listen and write.

MP3 HJ3-8

Garífuna Punta

Visitors to the ¹ _____ of Central America may find their feet moving to a beautifully entrancing beat. The music and ² _____ dance are called "punta," and they are a part of the special heritage of the Garífuna people.

The Garífuna developed punta music as a way to express their struggles and endurance over time. These days, traditional punta can be heard at parties and celebrations. It is even a part of wakes, a kind of ³ _____ celebration.

Key to punta are two drums made from ⁴ _____ out wood covered by the skin of a deer, sheep, or wild pig. These drums create the ⁵ _____ rhythm, with each drum playing a different beat. Other instruments include shakers and shells. There is also singing, with lyrics traditionally in the Garífuna language.

To dance punta, people move their feet and hips without moving their upper body. They make very small movements of their feet on the ground. They ⁶ _____ forward and back while keeping the feet flat, which shakes the knees, hips, and backside. The arms and hands may be lifted up going forward and placed down for backward movements.

In the past few decades, a new fusion form of punta has developed, called punta rock. It involves more instruments, and the lyrics may be in Spanish. However, traditional punta is still very much a part of Garífuna culture.

Word Bank

coasts	hollowed	rousing
rouzing	hallowed	acompanying
funeral	shufle	shuffle
funerel	costs	accompanying

Listen. Pause. Say each sentence.

MP3 HJ3-8G

Writing Practice

 Write the words.

1 _____

n land that touches the ocean

2 _____

adj going along with

3 _____

n a ceremony when someone dies

4 _____

adj made empty in the middle

5 _____

adj inspiring

6 _____

v walk with dragging feet

 Write the words in each blank.

Summary

"Punta," a music form and dance, is part of the _____ of the Garífuna people. It is a way to express struggles and endurance. Two _____ and other instruments create the rousing rhythm, and people sing traditional _____ in the Garífuna language. They also dance punta moving their feet and hips without moving their _____ body. A new fusion form of punta called "punta rock" has also developed.

Word Puzzle

 Complete the word puzzle.

Across

2 land that touches the ocean

4 a ceremony when someone dies

6 going along with

Down

1 made empty in the middle

3 walk with dragging feet

5 inspiring

The Mysterious Voynich Manuscript

 Teacher's Book p.230

The Voynich Manuscript is an extremely mysterious book. Its approximately 250 pages are filled with writing, but no one knows what language the words are written in. Inside the book are pictures of plants, but no one can figure out what species they are. So where did this book come from, and when was it made?

The manuscript gets its name from Wilfrid Voynich, a book dealer in Poland. He bought the book in 1912. However, it is thought that the book originally comes from Italy. Carbon dating on the manuscript revealed that the pages were likely created between the years 1404 and 1438.

For over a century, codebreakers and language experts from all over the world have attempted to find out what the writing system means. However, so far, no one has had any success. It is not sure if the writing is a natural language or a constructed language. One theory is that the language could have been from East Asia, but written in letters invented by the writer. Another theory is that the writing system is an invented code.

It is possible that the whole manuscript is a big trick and that the words have no meaning. However, increasingly sophisticated methods of analysis are starting to show that there is probably some sort of meaning to the writing. The secrets of the manuscript remain locked away. All we know is that this book has fascinated the world for over a hundred years.

CHAPTER 3

Technology

UNIT 9

Virtual Reality

Teacher's Book
p.231

List one pro and one con of virtual reality.

There are many amazing applications of virtual reality (VR), from training doctors to do surgery to helping students to immerse themselves in history. However, as is the case for any new technology, VR comes with ethical concerns.

One issue is that people who are able to do something in VR may think that their skill transfers to real life. Could people, and in particular children, believe that their fast motorcycle driving skills in virtual form would cross over to their regular life?

Another issue to consider is where it is appropriate for people to go in a virtual world. It is wonderful that VR gives people who are unable to travel the ability to see new worlds. But how limited should that world be? Would it be acceptable for a VR program to create a virtual copy of a celebrity's home, for example, and then let people walk around in it?

The question of physical versus psychological pain is also important. To what extent should pain, aggression, and violence be regulated in a virtual world? Could people undergo a type of psychological torture from VR, and if so, should this be controlled by laws?

These questions point to just a few of the many ethical issues related to technologies like virtual reality. However, history has shown that important discussions about the negative consequences of new technologies like VR are usually delayed until it is too late.

New Words

immerse yourself in	**ethical**
v get completely into	*adj* moral
undergo	**regulate**
v experience	*v* control
consequence	**delay**
n a result	*v* postpone

Part A. Picture Description

1.

His virtual reality goggles make him feel like he is _____ an underwater world.

(A) outside of
(B) immersed in
(C) looking up at
(D) flipping around

2.

✈STATUS

Flight JP452 to Madrid

Original departure:
3:00 PM

New expected
departure time: 3:30 PM

The flight has been _____.

(A) stopped
(B) delayed
(C) cancelled
(D) applauded

Part B. Sentence Completion

3. As is _____ for any new technology, there is some controversy around self-driving cars.

(A) case
(B) cases
(C) a case
(D) the case

4. _____ use this technology in schools?

(A) How is it do we
(B) Is appropriate we
(C) Is it appropriate to
(D) How appropriate it is

UNIT 9 Virtual Reality

The Miami Times

March 5, 2020

Many celebrities have started their own virtual reality (VR) rooms; now rapper 3 Linkz is the latest rapper to join in. Launched yesterday both online and through Simsang's offline VR headset, the VR room, which 3 Linkz has called "Link Crib," is a VR depiction of the rapper's own 7-bedroom mansion in Miami, Florida. Fans can explore the mansion while listening to songs from the latest album by 3 Linkz. The rap artist is also selling specialized VR goggles on his website at $38 a pair, with his personal logo on the side. Parents should be warned that the content is rated 16+.

5. What can users see in Link Crib?

(A) the headquarters of Simsang
(B) a live performance by 3 Linkz
(C) a VR version of a rapper's home
(D) a selection of different VR headsets

6. What can be inferred from the article?

(A) Link Crib is launching in April of 2020.
(B) The VR room can only be seen online.
(C) Link Crib contains obscene words or images.
(D) 3 Linkz's goggles are the current leading brand.

Part D. General Reading Comprehension

There are many amazing applications of virtual reality (VR), from training doctors to do surgery to helping students to immerse themselves in history. However, as is the case for any new technology, VR comes with ethical concerns.

One issue is that people who are able to do something in VR may think that their skill transfers to real life. Could people, and in particular children, believe that their fast motorcycle driving skills in virtual form would cross over to their regular life?

Another issue to consider is where it is appropriate for people to go in a virtual world. It is wonderful that VR gives people who are unable to travel the ability to see new worlds. But how limited should that world be? Would it be acceptable for a VR program to create a virtual copy of a celebrity's home, for example, and then let people walk around in it?

The question of physical versus psychological pain is also important. To what extent should pain, aggression, and violence be regulated in a virtual world? Could people undergo a type of psychological torture from VR, and if so, should this be controlled by laws?

These questions point to just a few of the many ethical issues related to technologies like virtual reality. However, history has shown that important discussions about the negative consequences of new technologies like VR are usually delayed until it is too late.

7. What would be the best title for the passage?

(A) Virtual Reality in the Medical Field
(B) The Pros and Cons of Virtual Reality
(C) Virtual Reality and Augmented Reality
(D) Ethical Issues Related to Virtual Reality

8. According to the passage, what VR problem may be worse for kids?

(A) worrying about their appearance
(B) getting rejected by friends in VR
(C) thinking that VR skills transfer to real life
(D) believing that colors in the real world are plain

9. Which of the following is NOT mentioned?

(A) traveling in a virtual world
(B) pedestrians in traffic accidents
(C) laws about psychological torture
(D) virtually copying a famous person's home

10. Which of these statements best matches the conclusion?

(A) The benefits of VR outweigh the drawbacks.
(B) People can learn more about history if they use VR.
(C) VR is likely to become a part of daily life for most people.
(D) Important decisions about VR will probably be postponed.

 Listen and write.

  MP3 HJ3-9

Virtual Reality

There are many amazing applications of virtual reality (VR), from training doctors to do surgery to helping students to ___¹___ themselves in history. However, as is the case for any new technology, VR comes with ethical concerns.

One issue is that people who are able to do something in VR may think that their skill transfers to real life. Could people, and in particular children, believe that their fast motorcycle driving skills in virtual form would cross over to their regular life?

Another issue to consider is where it is appropriate for people to go in a virtual world. It is wonderful that VR gives people who are unable to travel the ability to see new worlds. But how limited should that world be? Would it be acceptable for a VR program to create a virtual copy of a celebrity's home, for example, and then let people walk around in it?

The question of physical versus psychological pain is also important. To what extent should pain, aggression, and violence be ___²___ in a virtual world? Could people ___³___ a type of psychological torture from VR, and if so, should this be controlled by laws?

These questions point to just a few of the many ___⁴___ issues related to technologies like virtual reality. However, history has shown that important discussions about the negative ___⁵___ of new technologies like VR are usually ___⁶___ until it is too late.

Word Bank

regulated	consequences	ethecal
imerse	regulate	immerse
undergo	consequence	delayed
delaid	undergow	ethical

TOSEL
(H)

 Listen. Pause. Say each sentence.

 MP3 HJ3-9G

Writing Practice

Write the words.

1 _____

   [v] get completely into

2 _____

   [adj] moral

3 _____

   [v] experience

4 _____

   [v] control

5 _____

   [n] a result

6 _____

   [v] postpone

Write the words in each blank.

Summary

There are many amazing applications of virtual reality (VR), but this technology comes with _____ concerns. One issue is that people who are able to do something in VR may think that their skill transfers to _____ life. Another issue is about where people should be _____ to go in VR. In addition, the question of _____ versus psychological pain is important.

Word Puzzle

 Complete the word puzzle.

Across

1 experience

5 moral

6 a result

Down

2 control

3 get completely into

4 postpone

UNIT 10

Suspension Bridges

Teacher's Book
p.236

The picture shows a suspension bridge.
How do you think engineers ensure safety
when designing suspension bridges?

Suspension bridges work by suspending a road between two towers using connecting cables. The towers support the weight of the roadway and vehicles by compressing forces through the cables into the ground. Although such bridges have been in existence for around 500 years, the modern versions have a number of features that make these elegant bridges safer than earlier versions.

One way in which suspension bridges have improved over time is in how the main and supporting cables are constructed. In early times, the main cables were links of chain. When one of the links broke, the entire bridge would collapse. In modern suspension bridges, support cables are made out of high-strength steel. There are more support cables now than in early bridges, meaning that even if one cable fails, the bridge can still stand.

Another improvement over time is the stability of the bridge deck—the roadway itself. In the past, this deck tended to be unstable. In strong winds, the deck would shake so much that it fell apart. Modern bridges, on the other hand, have stiff decks that will not simply shake apart.

Unlike the Incas, who made impressive suspension bridges of twisted grass in the Andes mountains, modern suspension bridge designers incorporate strong metals into their work for sturdy, stable bridges. Nevertheless, a walk across a suspension bridge today is still an exhilarating experience.

New Words

suspend *v* hang	**cable** *n* a very thick rope of wire
vehicle *n* a car or truck	**collapse** *v* fall apart
chain *n* a series of linked parts	**exhilarating** *adj* very exciting

Part A. Picture Description

1.

The bridge is suspended via _____.

(A) steel cables
(B) linked chain
(C) twisted grass
(D) wooden blocks

2.

They are finding the experience _____.

(A) boring
(B) mediocre
(C) uninspiring
(D) exhilarating

Part B. Sentence Completion

3. _____ to ancient bridges, modern bridges are quite safe.

(A) Compared
(B) Comparing
(C) In compare
(D) If we comparing

4. Early bridges used to shake a lot. Modern bridges, _____, are relatively stable.

(A) whereas
(B) although
(C) in conclusion
(D) on the other hand

Akashi-Kaikyo Bridge: Japan

- almost 2 million workers
- 3,911m overall / 1,991m central span bridge deck
- around 10 years of construction
- cost Japanese ¥ 500 billion ($US 3.6 billion) to make it
- approximately 25,000 vehicles go over it daily
- strongest, longest, most expensive bridge in the world
- located in a typhoon region: wind speeds can be up to 290km/hr
- an accumulated total of 300,000km of cable
- 1,737 illumination lights

5. How long did it take to make the bridge?

(A) around a year
(B) about a decade
(C) approximately two decades
(D) almost half a century

6. Which of the following is true?

(A) There are over 2,000 lights on the bridge.
(B) The total length of the bridge is almost 4km.
(C) The bridge comprises 300,000 individual cables.
(D) It cost 3.6 billion Japanese yen to make the bridge.

Part D. General Reading Comprehension

Suspension bridges work by suspending a road between two towers using connecting cables. The towers support the weight of the roadway and vehicles by compressing forces through the cables into the ground. Although such bridges have been in existence for around 500 years, the modern versions have a number of features that make these elegant bridges safer than earlier versions.

One way in which suspension bridges have improved over time is in how the main and supporting cables are constructed. In early times, the main cables were links of chain. When one of the links broke, the entire bridge would collapse. In modern suspension bridges, support cables are made out of high-strength steel. There are more support cables now than in early bridges, meaning that even if one cable fails, the bridge can still stand.

Another improvement over time is the stability of the bridge deck—the roadway itself. In the past, this deck tended to be unstable. In strong winds, the deck would shake so much that it fell apart. Modern bridges, on the other hand, have stiff decks that will not simply shake apart.

Unlike the Incas, who made impressive suspension bridges of twisted grass in the Andes mountains, modern suspension bridge designers incorporate strong metals into their work for sturdy, stable bridges. Nevertheless, a walk across a suspension bridge today is still an exhilarating experience.

7. What is the main idea of the passage?

(A) Suspension bridges have become safer over time.
(B) Suspension bridges are the least stable type of bridge.
(C) Suspension bridges have existed for hundreds of years.
(D) Suspension bridges are unlikely to be used in the future.

8. According to the passage, what were early main cables made of?

(A) mud
(B) steel
(C) chain links
(D) twisted leather

9. What is the roadway between towers called?

(A) the deck
(B) the truss
(C) the stable
(D) the compressor

10. Which of the following is NOT mentioned as a feature of modern suspension bridges?

(A) two towers
(B) lookout windows
(C) sturdier materials
(D) more support cables

Listen and write.

  MP3 HJ3-10

Suspension Bridges

Suspension bridges work by ¹_____ a road between two towers using connecting cables. The towers support the weight of the roadway and ²_____ by compressing forces through the cables into the ground. Although such bridges have been in existence for around 500 years, the modern versions have a number of features that make these elegant bridges safer than earlier versions.

One way in which suspension bridges have improved over time is in how the main and supporting ³_____ are constructed. In early times, the main cables were links of ⁴_____. When one of the links broke, the entire bridge would ⁵_____. In modern suspension bridges, support cables are made out of high-strength steel. There are more support cables now than in early bridges, meaning that even if one cable fails, the bridge can still stand.

Another improvement over time is the stability of the bridge deck—the roadway itself. In the past, this deck tended to be unstable. In strong winds, the deck would shake so much that it fell apart. Modern bridges, on the other hand, have stiff decks that will not simply shake apart. Unlike the Incas, who made impressive suspension bridges of twisted grass in the Andes mountains, modern suspension bridge designers incorporate strong metals into their work for sturdy, stable bridges. Nevertheless, a walk across a suspension bridge today is still an ⁶_____ experience.

Word Bank

cabels	cables	collapse
vehicles	chain	suspending
suspenting	exilarating	colapse
exhilarating	veicles	chained

 Listen. Pause. Say each sentence.

  MP3 HJ3-10G

Writing Practice

 Write the words.

1 _____

v hang

2 _____

n a very thick rope of wire

3 _____

n a car or truck

4 _____

v fall apart

5 _____

n a series of linked parts

6 _____

adj very exciting

 Write the words in each blank.

Summary

Suspension bridges suspend a road between two towers using connecting cables. There are many _____ that have made these bridges safer over time. First, engineers now use high-_____ steel and more support cables than earlier versions. Secondly, suspension bridges now have stiff decks for _____. Nevertheless, a walk across a suspension bridge today is still an _____ experience.

Word Puzzle

 Complete the word puzzle.

Across

2 fall apart

4 a series of linked parts

5 a very thick rope of wire

6 a car or truck

Down

1 hang

3 very exciting

UNIT 11

Teacher's Book
p.242

Bone Conduction

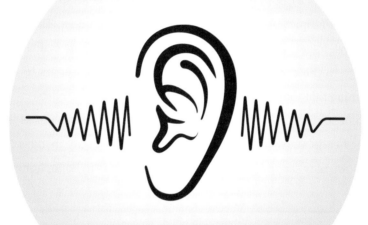

What are some of the downsides of using earphones?

Bone conduction is the movement of sound to the inner ear through the bones of one's skull. Technology using bone conduction is not new; the almost-deaf conductor Beethoven would put his conductor baton between his mouth and his piano to conduct sound to his ear. However, it is only in recent years that technologies with bone conduction have been refined. Recently, conventional headphones that conduct air have been joined on the market by bone conduction "bonephones."

The way bonephones work is simple. Rather than passing air through the eardrums, the device decodes sound waves by passing them through the jawbones and cheekbones and then converting them into vibration signals. The vibrations bypass the outer and middle ear and pass directly to the inner ear.

There are many benefits to bonephones. First, they can be adapted for underwater use. Nowadays, there are multiple devices that can be used by swimmers. There are even some for scuba divers that work meters underwater. In addition, there is some evidence that bonephones may reduce damage to the ears. Moreover, bonephones allow listeners to hear other sounds around them, meaning that they could be safer for pedestrians and cyclists.

Although the current sound quality of bone-conducting headphones is not as good as that of the best air-conducting headphones, improvements to the technology are made each year. As the 21st century progresses, we may see some remarkable developments in bonephones.

New Words

conduct	skull
v transmit	*n* the skeleton of a head
decode	conventional
v convert into a different, usable form	*adj* traditional
vibration	bypass
n a trembling	*v* go around

Part A. Picture Description

1.

The arrow is pointing to the _____.

(A) jawbone
(B) cheekbone
(C) wrist bone
(D) ankle bone

2.

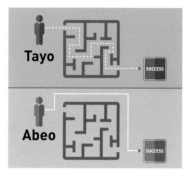

Unlike Tayo, Abeo decided to _____ the maze.

(A) bypass
(B) redraw
(C) go through
(D) pass through

Part B. Sentence Completion

3. It is only in recent years _____ system has been refined.

(A) this is
(B) for this
(C) when it
(D) that this

4. There _____ evidence that this technology is beneficial to swimmers.

(A) is some
(B) are some
(C) aren't an
(D) aren't the

Best Headphones June 2020

Model	Features	Cost
Audioconducts	Noise-cancelling air conduction over-the-ear headphones. Sure, it's not as elegant as an ultraportable in-ear set of buds, but the sound is professional quality (unlike with bonephones). The comfortable design makes them great for a commute.	$$$
Limemints	Leading the market in general bonephones. Titanium band and silicone coating makes this very flexible. Comes in 5 bright colors. Sweatproof. Wireless. Absence of noise cancellation means cyclists can hear cars. Up to six hours without being recharged (although charging is on the slow side).	$$$
VibeQuotients	Wireless earbuds. Excellent sound quality (although they're not noise-cancelling). Their superb fit and high water-resistance make these great for heavy-duty workouts. On a single two-hour charge, the rechargeable battery lasts 11 hours minimum. Not suitable for ocean swimming.	$$
Swimbones	Great set of bonephones for swimmers. Instead of loose earbuds, these clip-ons stay tight on top of your ears. Sound quality is only okay. 4GB of storage. Lithium-ion battery is rechargeable.	$$

$$$ (expensive) / $$ (a bit costly) / $ (affordable)

5. Which product would best suit a fitness fan who spends full days away from a charger?

   (A) Audioconducts
   (B) Limemints
   (C) VibeQuotients
   (D) Swimbones

6. Which of the following is true about the products?

   (A) Swimbones fit inside the inner ear.
   (B) VibeQuotients are suitable for ocean diving.
   (C) Audioconducts offer users noise cancellation.
   (D) Limemints are much less costly than Swimbones.

Bone conduction is the movement of sound to the inner ear through the bones of one's skull. Technology using bone conduction is not new; the almost-deaf conductor Beethoven would put his conductor baton between his mouth and his piano to conduct sound to his ear. However, it is only in recent years that technologies with bone conduction have been refined. Recently, conventional headphones that conduct air have been joined on the market by bone conduction "bonephones."

The way bonephones work is simple. Rather than passing air through the eardrums, the device decodes sound waves by passing them through the jawbones and cheekbones and then converting them into vibration signals. The vibrations bypass the outer and middle ear and pass directly to the inner ear.

There are many benefits to bonephones. First, they can be adapted for underwater use. Nowadays, there are multiple devices that can be used by swimmers. There are even some for scuba divers that work meters underwater. In addition, there is some evidence that bonephones may reduce damage to the ears. Moreover, bonephones allow listeners to hear other sounds around them, meaning that they could be safer for pedestrians and cyclists.

Although the current sound quality of bone-conducting headphones is not as good as that of the best air-conducting headphones, improvements to the technology are made each year. As the 21st century progresses, we may see some remarkable developments in bonephones.

7. What would be the best title for the passage?

(A) Hearing in Your Head: Bonephones
(B) It's in the Ear: Being a Better Composer
(C) Techniques: How Does Air Conduction Work?
(D) Noise-cancelling Headphones: Modern Worry?

8. According to the passage, what did Beethoven do?

(A) sit on top of his piano to compose songs
(B) use his conductor baton to receive sound
(C) put his head under his piano to hear sounds
(D) conduct by waving his conductor baton in both hands

9. Where does sound NOT pass through in bone conduction?

(A) the jawbone
(B) the inner ear
(C) the middle ear
(D) the cheekbones

10. What is listed as a disadvantage of bonephones compared to conventional headphones?

(A) They do not work underwater.
(B) They have worse sound quality.
(C) They increase damage to the ears.
(D) They are more dangerous to walk with.

UNIT 11 Bone Conduction

Listening Practice

 Listen and write.

  MP3 HJ3-11

Bone Conduction

Bone conduction is the movement of sound to the inner ear through the bones of one's
[1_____] . Technology using bone conduction is not new; the almost-deaf
conductor Beethoven would put his conductor baton between his mouth and his piano to
[2_____] sound to his ear. However, it is only in recent years that technologies with
bone conduction have been refined. Recently, [3_____] headphones that conduct
air have been joined on the market by bone conduction "bonephones."

The way bonephones work is simple. Rather than passing air through the eardrums, the device
[4_____] sound waves by passing them through the jawbones and cheekbones and
then converting them into [5_____] signals. The vibrations [6_____]
the outer and middle ear and pass directly to the inner ear.

There are many benefits to bonephones. First, they can be adapted for underwater use.
Nowadays, there are multiple devices that can be used by swimmers. There are even some for
scuba divers that work meters underwater. In addition, there is some evidence that bonephones
may reduce damage to the ears. Moreover, bonephones allow listeners to hear other sounds
around them, meaning that they could be safer for pedestrians and cyclists.

Although the current sound quality of bone-conducting headphones is not as good as that of the
best air-conducting headphones, improvements to the technology are made each year. As the 21st
century progresses, we may see some remarkable developments in bonephones.

Word Bank

scull	bypasses	decodes
conduction	decode	conduct
bypass	vibration	conventional
skull	conbentional	bivration

 Listen. Pause. Say each sentence.

  MP3 HJ3-11G

Writing Practice

 Write the words.

1 _____

v transmit

2 _____

n the skeleton of a head

3 _____

v convert into a different, usable form

4 _____

adj traditional

5 _____

n a trembling

6 _____

v go around

 Write the words in each blank.

Summary

Bone _____ is the movement of sound to the inner ear through the bones of one's _____. Technologies using bone conduction are not new but have been refined only recently. There are _____ called "bonephones" that conduct sound by bone conduction. The way bonephones _____ is simple, and there are many benefits to bonephones. As the 21st century progresses, we may see some remarkable developments in bonephones.

Word Puzzle

 Complete the word puzzle.

Across

2 go around

4 traditional

5 transmit

Down

1 a trembling

3 the skeleton of a head

6 convert into a different, usable form

Teacher's Book
p.249

UNIT 12

Videophones

How do you prefer to talk to friends:
1) in person?
2) over the phone (voice only)?
3) through video?

UNIT 12 Videophones

It is often thought that people will be excited to see any modern technology that has better capabilities than previous versions. However, as the developers of the first videophones discovered, this is not always the case.

While talking to someone through video is no shock to most people in modern times, back in the late 1920s, nothing like it had ever been seen. At that time, prototypes were being built in both New York City and Washington, D.C. for a device that would combine telephone and television. By the 1970s, one corporation had figured out how to make it work and was offering the service. However, the service had very few buyers.

One reason for the low interest was because the cost was so expensive. To sign up for the service, consumers needed to pay 90 US dollars a month, equivalent to around 700 US dollars in today's money. Most people could not afford this kind of luxury.

However, even among people who could pay, interest in the device was low. The company discovered through market research that a lot of people simply did not want to be seen while they were talking on the phone. In the end, it became apparent that people simply were not ready for or interested in this kind of technology. As this case shows, creating a technology will not always make people at the time want to use it.

New Words

capability	prototype
n the power to do something	*n* a first version of a device
figure out	sign up for
v determine	*v* register for
consumer	equivalent to
n a buyer	*adj* the same as

Part A. Picture Description

1.

As _____, they have a lot of choices in this supermarket.

(A) cashiers
(B) pioneers
(C) producers
(D) consumers

2.

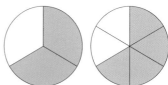

Figure A   **Figure B**

The total amount in figure A is _____ the total amount in figure B.

(A) bigger than
(B) smaller than
(C) starting from
(D) equivalent to

Part B. Sentence Completion

3. This phone has _____ capabilities than previous versions.

(A) many as
(B) many much
(C) as many as
(D) much better

4. Thirty years ago, most people could not afford _____ a microwave oven.

(A) buy
(B) to buy
(C) they bought
(D) have bought

AROMAVISION

It's TV that you can smell!
Simply plug the patented Aromavision-StickTM into your TV and you can enjoy immersing yourself in the scents of the setting you see on TV.

Is the hero in a rainforest? Why not smell the beautiful scent of trees?
Is there a battle on a pirate ship? Don't just hear the roar of the waves—feel like you're there with the salty smell of the ocean!

Call 1-555-894-0187 toll free or
go to www.aromavision.internet TODAY
to find out how you can get Aromavision in your home.
Smell like you're there with Aromavision!

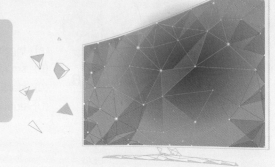

5. What is the main purpose of Aromavision?

   (A) to provide a clearer visual screen image
   (B) to help people with a poor sense of smell
   (C) to offer soothing scents as a form of therapy
   (D) to aid viewers in feeling immersed in a scene

6. How can people use Aromavision?

   (A) by wearing a virtual reality headset
   (B) by paying for a monthly TV subscription
   (C) by inserting a product into their television set
   (D) by installing a specially patented TV in their home

Part D. General Reading Comprehension

It is often thought that people will be excited to see any modern technology that has better capabilities than previous versions. However, as the developers of the first videophones discovered, this is not always the case.

While talking to someone through video is no shock to most people in modern times, back in the late 1920s, nothing like it had ever been seen. At that time, prototypes were being built in both New York City and Washington, D.C. for a device that would combine telephone and television. By the 1970s, one corporation had figured out how to make it work and was offering the service. However, the service had very few buyers.

One reason for the low interest was because the cost was so expensive. To sign up for the service, consumers needed to pay 90 US dollars a month, equivalent to around 700 US dollars in today's money. Most people could not afford this kind of luxury.

However, even among people who could pay, interest in the device was low. The company discovered through market research that a lot of people simply did not want to be seen while they were talking on the phone. In the end, it became apparent that people simply were not ready for or interested in this kind of technology. As this case shows, creating a technology will not always make people at the time want to use it.

7. What is the passage mainly about?

(A) the invention of television
(B) public shock at the first telephone
(C) people's initial reactions to 3D screens
(D) the unwanted technology of videophones

8. According to the passage, when were prototypes for videophones first built?

(A) in the 1920s
(B) in the 1950s
(C) in the 1970s
(D) in the 1990s

9. What is one reason mentioned for low interest in videophones?

(A) a concern about attacks by robbers
(B) a desire not to be seen while talking
(C) a worry that the technology looked cheap
(D) a dislike of the way the videophones looked

10. According to the writer, what lesson can be learned from the case of videophones?

(A) Not every new technology is wanted by the public.
(B) Talking to people face-to-face is better than over a phone.
(C) New technologies start out expensive but get cheaper over time.
(D) Teaching young people to use technologies is important for the future.

Listen and write.

  MP3 HJ3-12

Videophones

It is often thought that people will be excited to see any modern technology that has better

[1 _____] than previous versions. However, as the developers of the first

videophones discovered, this is not always the case.

While talking to someone through video is no shock to most people in modern times, back in the

late 1920s, nothing like it had ever been seen. At that time, [2 _____] were being

built in both New York City and Washington, D.C. for a device that would combine telephone

and television. By the 1970s, one corporation had [3 _____] out how to make it work

and was offering the service. However, the service had very few buyers.

One reason for the low interest was because the cost was so expensive. To [4 _____]

up for the service, [5 _____] needed to pay 90 US dollars a month,

[6 _____] to around 700 US dollars in today's money. Most people could not afford

this kind of luxury.

However, even among people who could pay, interest in the device was low. The company

discovered through market research that a lot of people simply did not want to be seen while

they were talking on the phone. In the end, it became apparent that people simply were not

ready for or interested in this kind of technology. As this case shows, creating a technology will

not always make people at the time want to use it.

Word Bank

be signed	consumers	prototypes
capabilities	cunsumers	figured
figure	sign	equivalent
capavilities	prototips	equivlent

TOSEL
H

 Listen. Pause. Say each sentence.

  MP3 HJ3-12G

Writing Practice

 Write the words.

1 _____	2 _____
n the power to do something	*n* a first version of a device
3 _____	4 _____
v determine	*v* register for
5 _____	6 _____
n a buyer	*adj* the same as

 Write the words in each blank.

Summary

Creating a _____ does not always make people want to see it at that time. One good

example is the _____. When it was first _____, use of the device was

low because it was so _____ and people simply were not interested in using this kind

of technology.

Word Puzzle

 Complete the word puzzle.

Across

1 register for

3 a buyer

5 the power to do something

6 determine

Down

2 a first version of a device

4 the same as

The Antikythera Mechanism: An Ancient Machine

Teacher's Book p.254

Long before the modern computer there was the Antikythera Mechanism. This ancient Greek technological tool, thought to be from the first or second century BCE, is known by some as the world's first analog computer.

The mechanism was found by divers in 1900. It was in a wooden box in the Mediterranean Sea, among many other artifacts in a shipwreck near a Greek island. The machine is made of bronze parts, and probably once had 37 gears. It has some instructions on it written in ancient Greek. It shows the Greek zodiac and the Egyptian 365-day calendar. It also shows the Sun, the Moon, and the five planets that the ancient Greeks knew about. It is not known why it was being transported by ship, but it is thought that it had been stolen and was being taken to Rome for a parade for the emperor, Julius Caesar.

The Antikythera Mechanism was probably used as a calendar and to predict eclipses and the positions of the planets and stars. It was likely also used to track the times for ancient Greek games such as the Olympics. However, as technology develops, new discoveries about the mechanism are always being found. In the meantime, this incredible machine of the ancient world continues to mystify and enthrall the world.

Antikythera

ANSWERS

CHAPTER 1 | Social Studies / Psychology

p.10

UNIT 1
HJ3-1
p.11

1 (B)	2 (B)	3 (B)	4 (C)	5 (D)	6 (C)	7 (B)	8 (D)	9 (B)	10 (D)

🎧 1 monarchy 2 ruler 3 officials 4 citizens 5 elected 6 democracy

✏️ 1 monarchy 2 ruler 3 elect 4 official 5 democracy 6 citizen

📄 parent, democracy, vote, parliamentary

→ 3 monarchy 5 citizen 6 ruler ↓ 1 democracy 2 elect 4 official

UNIT 2
HJ3-2
p.19

1 (C)	2 (C)	3 (A)	4 (A)	5 (D)	6 (A)	7 (C)	8 (A)	9 (D)	10 (B)

🎧 1 rush hour 2 earnings 3 commuters 4 appreciated 5 driven 6 cautious

✏️ 1 rush hour 2 commuter 3 earnings 4 driven by 5 appreciate 6 cautious

📄 violinist, busker, purpose, appreciated

→ 2 commuter 4 driven by 5 cautious 6 rush hour ↓ 1 appreciate 3 earnings

UNIT 3
HJ3-3
p.27

1 (B)	2 (C)	3 (C)	4 (B)	5 (C)	6 (A)	7 (B)	8 (D)	9 (D)	10 (D)

🎧 1 copyright 2 permission 3 pesticides 4 property 5 patent 6 Activists

✏️ 1 copyright 2 permission 3 pesticide 4 property 5 patent 6 activist

📄 traditional, India, properties, battle

→ 1 permission 4 copyright 5 patent ↓ 1 pesticide 2 property 3 activist

UNIT 4
HJ3-4
p.35

1 (C)	2 (B)	3 (C)	4 (D)	5 (B)	6 (C)	7 (B)	8 (A)	9 (D)	10 (A)

🎧 1 psychology 2 motivates 3 belonging 4 self-esteem 5 claims 6 prioritize

✏️ 1 psychology 2 motivate 3 self-esteem 4 claim 5 belonging 6 prioritize

📄 Hierarchy, popular, biology, motivation

→ 4 prioritize 5 motivate ↓ 1 self-esteem 2 claim 3 belonging 4 psychology

CHAPTER 2 | Culture

p.44

UNIT 5
HJ3-5
p.45

1 (B)	2 (A)	3 (A)	4 (B)	5 (B)	6 (C)	7 (C)	8 (A)	9 (D)	10 (D)

🎧 1 folklore 2 mythological 3 beasts 4 hybrids 5 vicious 6 scales

✏️ 1 folklore 2 beast 3 mythological 4 hybrid 5 vicious 6 scales

📄 mythological, hybrids, beasts, link

→ 5 mythological 6 beast ↓ 1 vicious 2 hybrid 3 folklore 4 scales

UNIT 6
HJ3-6
p.53

1 (A)	2 (A)	3 (C)	4 (C)	5 (A)	6 (C)	7 (C)	8 (C)	9 (B)	10 (D)

🎧 1 holiest 2 rituals 3 fast 4 dusk 5 sip 6 loved

✏️ 1 holy 2 ritual 3 fast 4 dusk 5 sip of 6 loved ones

📄 religion, rituals, fast, three

→ 1 holy 3 dusk 4 sip of 6 ritual ↓ 2 loved ones 5 fast

UNIT 7
HJ3-7
p.61

1 (C)	2 (C)	3 (C)	4 (A)	5 (D)	6 (C)	7 (A)	8 (D)	9 (A)	10 (A)

🎧 1 delight 2 population 3 access 4 portable 5 loaded it up 6 alternatives

✏️ 1 delight 2 population 3 portable 4 access to 5 load 6 alternative

📄 population, retired, modified, alternatives

→ 2 alternative 3 population 6 portable ↓ 1 delight 4 access to 5 load up with

UNIT 8
HJ3-8
p.69

1 (D)	2 (B)	3 (B)	4 (D)	5 (D)	6 (C)	7 (B)	8 (C)	9 (B)	10 (C)

🎧 1 coasts 2 accompanying 3 funeral 4 hollowed 5 rousing 6 shuffle

✏️ 1 coast 2 accompanying 3 funeral 4 hollowed out 5 rousing 6 shuffle

📄 heritage, drums, songs, upper

→ 2 coast 4 funeral 6 accompanying ↓ 1 hollowed out 3 shuffle 5 rousing

CHAPTER 3 | Technology

p.78

UNIT 9
HJ3-9
p.79

1 (B)	2 (B)	3 (D)	4 (C)	5 (C)	6 (C)	7 (D)	8 (C)	9 (B)	10 (D)

🎧 1 immerse 2 regulated 3 undergo 4 ethical 5 consequences 6 delayed

✏️ 1 immerse yourself in 2 ethical 3 undergo 4 regulate 5 consequence 6 delay

📄 ethical, real, allowed, physical

→ 1 undergo 5 ethical 6 consequence ↓ 2 regulate 3 immerse yourself in 4 delay

UNIT 10
HJ3-10
p.87

1 (A)	2 (D)	3 (A)	4 (D)	5 (B)	6 (B)	7 (A)	8 (C)	9 (A)	10 (B)

🎧 1 suspending 2 vehicles 3 cables 4 chain 5 collapse 6 exhilarating

✏️ 1 suspend 2 cable 3 vehicle 4 collapse 5 chain 6 exhilarating

📄 features, strength, stability, exhilarating

→ 2 collapse 4 chain 5 cable 6 vehicle ↓ 1 suspend 3 exhilarating

UNIT 11
HJ3-11
p.95

1 (A)	2 (A)	3 (D)	4 (A)	5 (C)	6 (C)	7 (A)	8 (B)	9 (C)	10 (B)

🎧 1 skull 2 conduct 3 conventional 4 decodes 5 vibration 6 bypass

✏️ 1 conduct 2 skull 3 decode 4 conventional 5 vibration 6 bypass

📄 conduction, skull, headphones, work

→ 2 bypass 4 conventional 5 conduct ↓ 1 vibration 3 skull 6 decode

UNIT 12
HJ3-12
p.103

1 (D)	2 (D)	3 (D)	4 (B)	5 (D)	6 (C)	7 (D)	8 (A)	9 (B)	10 (A)

🎧 1 capabilities 2 prototypes 3 figured 4 sign 5 consumers 6 equivalent

✏️ 1 capability 2 prototype 3 figure out 4 sign up for 5 consumer 6 equivalent to

📄 technology, videophone, introduced, expensive

→ 1 sign up for 3 consumer 5 capability 6 figure out ↓ 2 prototype 4 equivalent to